KOREAN WAR

ABDO
Publishing Company

KOREAN WAR

BY SHANNON BAKER MOORE

CONTENT CONSULTANT

George L. Kallander
Associate Professor of History, Syracuse University

CREDITS

Published by ABDO Publishing Company, PO Box 398166, Minneapolis, MN 55439. Copyright © 2014 by Abdo Consulting Group, Inc. International copyrights reserved in all countries. No part of this book may be reproduced in any form without written permission from the publisher. The Essential Library™ is a trademark and logo of ABDO Publishing Company.

Printed in the United States of America,
North Mankato, Minnesota
052013
112013

 THIS BOOK CONTAINS AT LEAST 10% RECYCLED MATERIALS.

Editor: Lauren Coss
Series Designer: Emily Love

Photo Credits
AP Images, cover, 2, 11, 33, 36, 39, 49, 62, 68, 74, 76, 80, 87, 88, 91, 99 (left), 99 (right), 101; Bettmann/Corbis/ AP Images, 6, 17, 46, 55, 98 (left); Topical Press Agency/Getty Images, 18; Charles Gorry/AP Images, 23, 101; Korean Central News Agency/AP Images, 26, 28, 101; Henry Burroughs/AP Images, 35; Korean Central News Agency/Korea News Service/AP Images, 43; Max Desfor/AP Images, 51, 98 (right); William C. Allen/AP Images, 56; SS/AP Images, 60; Frank Noel/AP Images, 64; Red Line Editorial, 71, 100, 101; Lissandra Melo/Shutterstock Images, 96

Library of Congress Control Number: 2013932675

Cataloging-in-Publication Data
Moore, Shannon Baker.
 Korean War / Shannon Baker Moore.
   p. cm. -- (Essential library of American wars)
Includes bibliographical references and index.
ISBN 978-1-61783-878-1
1. Korean War, 1950-1953--History--Juvenile literature. Korean War, 1950-1953--Korea--Juvenile literature. I. Title.
951.904--dc23

2013932675

CONTENTS

A BOLD PLAN

It was late summer in 1950. The Korean War was not going well for South Korea and its ally, the United Nations (UN). UN commanders feared they might lose the entire Korean Peninsula—and the war.

Five years earlier, near the end of World War II (1939–1945), the victorious Allied forces had divided the Korean Peninsula in two. North Korea had become a Communist country, allied with the Soviet Union and China. The United States had allied itself with South Korea, and it was determined to keep South Korea from falling to the Communists as well.

Then on June 25, 1950, the Korean People's Army (KPA) of North Korea launched a major assault against South Korea. The UN rushed in troops under the command of the United States to help South Korea. The UN force, known as the Eighth

In September 1950, US Marines led a daring amphibious assault on the South Korean port of Inchon, hoping to drive back North Korean forces.

THE UNITED NATIONS

The United Nations (UN) is an international organization established after World War II to help promote peace, international cooperation, human rights, and social progress. Throughout the Korean War, the United States played a strong role in leading the organization. During the war, UN member nations came to the aid of South Korea. Seventeen countries, including South Korea and the United States, provided combat units. Five countries provided medical support. More than 90 percent of UN troops came from South Korea and the United States.[1] The US military led the UN forces.

Army, had superior air and naval power. However, the North Koreans had better weapons on the ground and more soldiers. Their fighters were more experienced. For seven weeks, KPA forces pushed the Republic of Korea (ROK) Army and UN forces toward the coast.

By early August 1950, ROK and UN forces clung to a tiny southeastern corner of Korea known as the Pusan Perimeter. The sea lay behind them. There was nowhere else to go. But the war was not over yet. US lieutenant general Walton H. Walker led the Eighth Army and ROK forces trapped on the Pusan Perimeter. His troops had been able to maintain their position, but they could only hold off the constant North Korean attacks for so long. It was time for a bold plan to change the course of the war.

TAKING A RISK

US general Douglas MacArthur was known for his daring military maneuvers. MacArthur was the supreme commander of the UN forces. He had a plan. He would take part of Walker's troops and use them to launch a surprise attack behind enemy lines.

MacArthur proposed an amphibious landing at the port of Inchon, which was controlled by North Korea. UN air, naval, and infantry forces would attack North Korean forces on the coast. Then the UN forces would move inland. There, MacArthur hoped to retake the capital city of Seoul, South Korea, which had fallen to North Korea early in the war.

MacArthur's plan was known as Operation Chromite, and many thought it was extremely risky. One US Navy official said, "We drew up a list of every natural and geographic handicap—and Inchon had 'em all."[2] Even MacArthur admitted there was only a 1 in 5,000 chance his scheme would work.

THE CHALLENGES OF INCHON

Inchon was a poor place for an amphibious landing. A major danger was the extreme ocean tides. Inchon had some of the highest tides in the world. The water could rise as much as 33 feet (10 m), making a water landing extremely hazardous. None of the UN officers had experience operating in such high tides, and few had experience with amphibious landings. The extreme tides also created strong water currents, which made maneuvering ships difficult. The currents moved as fast as some of the small landing craft.

Before UN troops could invade Inchon, they would have to capture Wolmido, a small island at the mouth of the port. The enemy troops at Wolmido were fortified with 75mm guns. UN forces would need to destroy these guns. Otherwise, the UN's main landing force would be exposed to enemy fire. After Wolmido, UN ships would then need to slip through a dangerously narrow channel to get to Inchon. North Korean forces had planted explosive mines all along this narrow channel.

Even if UN forces made it past these dangers, the battle would be far from over. Fifteen-foot (4.6 m) seawalls surrounded the harbor at Inchon. The UN landing craft would need to approach during high tide in order to reach the seawalls. If they came when the tide was too low, the boats would get trapped in the mud that coated the shallow seafloor. After arriving, UN forces would have just two hours to get ashore and destroy

This map from 1950 shows South Korea at the time of the Inchon invasion. The arrows indicate areas where military action was reported.

enemy forces in the city before darkness fell. UN troops would have to leave their landing crafts and climb up the seawall using ladders. The troops would be exposed and vulnerable to enemy fire the entire time. Inchon was a large city with 250,000 people. Every house could hide the enemy.

If the mission failed, the UN troops would be trapped. Their boats would be stuck in the mud for 12 hours until the tide was high enough for them to escape. The UN troops at Inchon would not have any backup if MacArthur's strategy did not work as planned.

A DECISION IS REACHED

Back in Washington, DC, the Joint Chiefs of Staff, leaders of the US military, were skeptical of MacArthur's plan. General Omar Bradley, chairman of the Joint Chiefs of Staff, said, "It was the riskiest military proposal I had ever heard of. . . . Inchon was probably the worst possible place ever selected for an amphibious landing."[3]

However, MacArthur was famous for his military successes as a commander during World War II. He had a record of 56 successful amphibious assaults in the Pacific. Many people considered him a genius of military strategy. On August 23, 1950, MacArthur told US Navy leaders:

> *The enemy, I am convinced, has failed to prepare Inchon properly for defense. The very arguments you have made as to the impracticabilities involved will tend to ensure for me the element of surprise. For the enemy commander will reason that no one would be so brash as to make such an attempt. Surprise is the most vital element for success in war.*[4]

In spite of their misgivings, the Joint Chiefs ultimately agreed to MacArthur's plan. US Marines would lead the attack. To carry out the invasion, MacArthur took

WORLD WAR II AND THE RISE OF COMMUNISM

Many of the military leaders involved in the Korean War, including MacArthur, participated in World War II. In 1939, Germany's dictator Adolf Hitler seemed unstoppable. His Nazi forces took over many European nations. Italy and Japan joined with Germany to form what became known as the Axis powers. France, Great Britain, the United States, the Soviet Union, and China also joined together. This group became known as the Allied powers. After the Allies defeated Hitler and the Axis powers in 1945, the partnership among the Allied forces fell apart. Communist countries such as the Soviet Union and China were at odds with capitalist countries such as the United States and its allies.

part of Walker's army and formed a new unit, the Tenth Corps, known as the X Corps, which would be commanded by US general Edward M. Almond.

Led by the US military, the UN forces did everything possible to ensure the success of Operation Chromite. They staged phony attacks up and down the west coast of South Korea, hoping to hide the real attack from the North Koreans. For five days, UN naval gunfire and air strikes bombarded Wolmido. Navy ships cleared the channel of mines.

ASSAULT ON INCHON

On September 15, 1950, MacArthur watched from the flagship *Mount McKinley* as the 261 ships and 80,000 men of Operation Chromite prepared for attack.[5] The sky was thick with smoke, and

GENERAL DOUGLAS MACARTHUR

General Douglas MacArthur was known as a difficult man to say no to. He was a controversial US general who commanded in the Pacific during World War II. He had also commanded the Allied occupation of postwar Japan. MacArthur was known for being brilliant, but he was also seen as dramatic and even cocky. Many military leaders and civilians disliked him. MacArthur was known as a commander who did things his own way, at times breaking the rules when it suited him. He sometimes moved ahead without waiting for official approval.

the sound of roaring airplanes and booming naval guns filled the air.

The tides required a two-stage invasion. Stage one would take place during the high tide in the morning. Stage two would occur during high tide in the evening. At 6:33 a.m. on September 15, the X Corps began its assault on the island of Wolmido. UN airplanes flew in just ahead of the troops to provide air cover. The attack on the island went smoothly. With little enemy resistance, the island was secured in a little over an hour. Not a single UN soldier was killed. Stage one had been a success.

The UN forces waited a tense 12 hours for the next tide. Then they stormed Inchon. Crowding into small landing craft, the X Corps hit Red Beach and Blue Beach, code names for the landing sites. The first troops scaled the seawalls at 5:32 p.m. and attacked the city. Meeting little enemy resistance, they quickly captured the beachheads and sealed off the city. With the X Corps attacking from the rear, the North Koreans withdrew northward. Now General Walker could break out of the Pusan Perimeter. On September 16, 1950, the day after the invasion of Inchon, Walker and his troops began their offensive.

Walker's Eighth Army secured the nearby railroad and the main highway. Another important target was Kimpo airfield, the largest and most important airfield on the Korean Peninsula. On the night of September 17, US Marines attacked the airfield. By morning, it was completely under UN control. Now UN forces could use the airfield for their own fighter and bomber planes and could more easily attack North Korea.

The X Corps pushed northeast, hoping to drive the North Korean forces from the South Korean capital of Seoul. They reached the Han River on September 19. The next day, they advanced into the outskirts of the city. Here they clashed with 20,000 North Korean troops sent to reinforce the city.[6] The battle for Seoul was one of the most vicious of the entire war. From the invasion of Inchon to Seoul, the X Corps suffered 3,500 casualties, most in Seoul. Roughly 14,000 North Koreans soldiers were killed and 7,000 captured.[7]

A BRILLIANT VICTORY

As he had predicted, MacArthur's surprise attack was a complete success. Inchon fell in less than two days. Seoul was liberated on September 27, 1950, 12 days after the invasion of Inchon. On September 29, MacArthur turned the liberated

UN forces captured thousands of North Korean troops during the successful invasion of Inchon.

capital over to South Korean president Syngman Rhee. With the smell of victory in the air, MacArthur boasted he would wrap up the war by Thanksgiving and have the Eighth Army out of Korea by Christmas. He had no idea how wrong he was.

A DIVIDED NATION

The Korean War officially began in 1950, but tensions had been tearing the Korean Peninsula apart for decades before war broke out. In 1910, Korea had become a Japanese colony, and Japan tried to impose its culture, politics, economics, and even its language on Korea. The Japanese closed many Korean schools, limited the Koreans' freedoms, and forced many Koreans to labor in mines. Many Koreans resisted Japan's occupation. Other Koreans accepted the modern reforms and business practices of the Japanese.

CIVIL CONFLICT

Japan's dominance over Korea ended in 1945 with the Allied victory in World War II. The Allies had promised Koreans independence after the war. But Allied leaders felt the country was not ready to govern itself. Without input from Koreans, the United States split Korea in two near the line formed at latitude

When Korea became a Japanese colony, Japanese gendarmes, soldiers who acted as a police force, enforced strict laws on Koreans.

38° on the map. The division was known as the 38th parallel. The Soviet Union would occupy all territory north of the 38th parallel, and the United States would occupy the territory south of the line until Korea was ready to govern itself. In the meantime, the Allies set up temporary governments in the divided country—the United States in the South and the Soviet Union in the North.

The end of Japanese rule did not bring peace to the now-divided Korea. Both North and South were anxious for full independence, but people had different ideas about how the Korean Peninsula should be governed. Korea had a long history of peasant farmers working for rich landholders. Many poor Koreans felt these landholders unfairly held all the wealth and power in the country. There were different nationalist movements across the Korean Peninsula as it struggled for independence. Each movement had its own views about what was best for Korea. Many nationalist movements wanted the country to become Communist.

Fear of Communism was spreading in the United States. Many US leaders saw Communism as a threat to US capitalism. The Soviet Union was a powerful, heavily armed Communist dictatorship, and its influence and power seemed to be growing. Communists had also taken over China after a brutal civil war. Communism seemed to be spreading like wildfire.

US FEARS

The United States was determined to keep South Korea from becoming Communist. In May 1948, Rhee was elected as the head of the Republic of Korea. He was a well-known activist who had studied in the United States. US officials had made him a member of the temporary government in the South following World War II. The United States had mixed feelings about Rhee. He was known to be brutal and repressive. However, he was not a Communist, and that was most important to US officials.

Kim Il-Sung was a member of the temporary government the Soviet Union had set up in the

THE TRUMAN DOCTRINE

In an effort to prevent the spread of Communism, President Harry S. Truman declared the United States must "support free peoples who are resisting attempted subjugation by armed minorities or by outside pressures."[1] This statement, known as the Truman Doctrine, was a warning to the Soviet Union that the United States would help other countries if the Soviet Union threatened them.

northern half of Korea. Like many other nationalists, he wanted Korea to become a Communist country. By 1947, Kim had laid the groundwork for a Communist government in the North, with the help of the Soviet Union and many other groups. In September 1948, he became the leader of the Democratic People's Republic of Korea, the official name of North Korea. In December, the Soviets pulled out of the country after holding elections for a North Korean government. In June 1949, the United States withdrew its military from South Korea. Now both North and South Korea were independent.

TENSIONS MOUNT

Korea may have had two independent governments, but neither Rhee's nor Kim's government recognized the authority of the other. Both men wanted a unified Korea free from foreign

The United States considered Rhee, *right*, shown in 1948 with MacArthur, *left*, an ally because he did not have Communist ties.

domination, but they still disagreed about how the country should be run. Each wanted to control Korea's destiny, and each violently crushed others who opposed them. North Koreans and South Koreans often provoked one another, and skirmishes were common along the 38th parallel. More than 100,000 Koreans were killed before the war even started.[2]

Both the United States and the Soviet Union had left military advisers behind in their respective sides of Korea. Because Rhee repeatedly threatened to invade North Korea, the United States deliberately restricted military aid to South Korea. The Soviet Union, on the other hand, kept North Korea well supplied. The Soviets protected the North with an army of 135,000 troops, 120 Soviet T-34 tanks, heavy artillery, plus support from 180 Soviet aircraft and a few naval patrol craft.[3]

Rhee was not the only Korean leader threatening invasion. Kim wanted to invade South Korea and unify all Koreans into one Communist country. To gain support from North Koreans, he exposed the United States as an oppressive force in the South. In a speech given in May 1950, Kim said,

US RIVALRY WITH THE SOVIET UNION

"This Republic and its citizens . . . stand in their deepest peril."[4] This dire warning came in a top secret document given to President Truman on April 7, 1950. Known as *NSC-68*, the report detailed US military needs for the ongoing conflict with the Soviet Union known as the Cold War. The report said the Soviets wanted "to retain and solidify their absolute power."[5] The report then warned that US military power was inadequate. *NSC-68* stressed that the United States needed to quickly build up its military strength.

Korea, freed from the Japanese occupationers' oppression, has been artificially divided with the 38th parallel as the demarcation line, and the South Korean people find themselves again groaning under the rule of the foreign invaders, the US imperialists.[6]

KIM IL-SUNG

Kim Il-Sung was the son of parents who fled to Manchuria, China, to escape the Japanese occupation of Korea. While in Manchuria, Kim became a Communist and fought in the Manchurian guerrilla war against Japan. He later joined the Soviet army and was with them in 1945 as they prepared to attack the Japanese at the end of World War II.

KIM IL-SUNG SEEKS ALLIES

Kim believed he could unify the peninsula quickly without help from his Communist neighbors, but he still sought support from other Communist leaders, such as Joseph Stalin of the Soviet Union and Mao Zedong of China.

Kim's threats made the United States nervous. US leaders believed the Soviet Union was the mastermind behind the plans to invade South Korea. Some US officials worried Korea might even be a trap designed to pull in US forces so the Soviets

Kim Il-Sung

could successfully attack somewhere else in the world. In reality, Stalin was more concerned with events in Europe, and he was skeptical of Kim's plan. Kim worked hard to convince Stalin invading South Korea was a good idea. In April 1950, Stalin finally agreed to the invasion, but Stalin warned Kim that he should not count on help from the Soviet military.

As for Mao, China's civil war had barely ended. Communist China was only one year old, and Mao was still trying to solidify his own power. Although Mao's chief interest was at home, he still expressed his support for North Korea. North Korean fighters had supported Mao in his Communist revolution, and he felt indebted to them. He also knew the US-supported South Korea was hostile toward Communism. A South Korean takeover of the North would threaten Mao's regime. With the approval and moral support of Stalin and Mao, Kim was ready to strike.

NORTH KOREA ATTACKS

At 4:00 a.m. on June 25, 1950, North Korean troops launched a major assault against South Korea. John J. Muccio, the US ambassador to South Korea, sent an encoded message to the US State Department:

> North Korean forces invaded ROK territory at several points this morning. . . . Ongjin blasted by North Korean artillery fire. About six [a.m.] North Korean infantry commence crossing [38th] parallel in Ongjin area. . . . It would appear from nature of attack and manner in which it was launched it constitutes all out offensive against ROK.[7]

The Korean War had begun.

THE UNITED STATES STEPS IN

On June 25, 1950, US president Harry S. Truman was on vacation at his home in Independence, Missouri. At approximately 9:20 p.m., Truman's phone rang. It was Dean Acheson, the US secretary of state. Acheson was in charge of the State Department, the government agency in charge of US relations with other countries. "Mr. President, I have very serious news," Acheson said. "The North Koreans have invaded South Korea."[1]

Despite the ongoing hostilities within Korea, the attack caught US officials off guard. Acheson suggested Truman request a meeting of the UN Security Council, the senior governing group of the UN, to discuss the invasion. He believed many nations acting together would send a stronger

With North Korea's invasion of the South, the Korean War began.

signal than the United States acting alone. Truman agreed. Although the president had not yet returned to Washington, DC, Acheson called an emergency meeting of the UN Security Council. The council voted 9–0 to pass a resolution condemning the attack and calling on North Korea to withdraw. However, the resolution did not stop North Korea.

HARRY S. TRUMAN

Truman had been vice president for just 82 days when President Franklin D. Roosevelt died on April 12, 1945, passing the presidency to Truman. Truman was reelected in 1948. As president, Truman authorized the use of atomic bombs on Japan during World War II. He also established the Truman Doctrine, his plan for containing Communism. His presidency helped establish the UN, the Marshall Plan to aid postwar Europe, and the North Atlantic Treaty Organization (NATO). In 1948, he signed an executive order desegregating the US military.

NORTH KOREA GAINING

The KPA was quickly taking over the entire Korean Peninsula, and Rhee requested help from the United States. On June 27, Truman ordered air and naval strikes against the North Koreans.

That same day, the North Koreans stormed into Seoul with their Soviet T-34 tanks. Rhee and his government evacuated to

Pusan, southeast of Seoul, to avoid capture. Refugees and South Korean troops streamed southward. With the government and military fleeing, there was nothing to stop the North Korean advance.

On June 27, the United States submitted a new resolution to the UN, calling for its members to help South Korea repel the North Korean attack. Since most of the troops helping South Korea would come from the United States, the United States wanted to lead the UN forces. While the UN considered the resolution, the first US ground troops, known as Task Force Smith, arrived in Korea on July 1. Their orders were to "contact the enemy and delay his advance."[2] The North Korean offensive was pushing rapidly southward, and it would take time to get more troops, tanks,

TASK FORCE SMITH

Task Force Smith consisted of 540 US troops.[4] Most of the men in Task Force Smith were green, meaning they had never seen combat. Their average age was 20. Because military spending had been drastically cut after World War II, many US soldiers did not have proper training or equipment. The South Korean forces were no better prepared and even younger. Later in the war, ROK forces were often teenage boys picked up off the street. South Korean police roamed the streets hunting for any man or boy capable of fighting. Then they gave each one a few hours of training and sent him into battle.

and artillery from the United States to South Korea.

THE FIGHTING BEGINS

By July 5, Task Force Smith had set up a defensive position south of Seoul near the city of Osan, South Korea. Soon they saw the enemy—T-34 tanks. The US troops were unprepared to fight. One Task Force Smith soldier said,

At any one time it seems like there'd be four tanks behind us curling up the hill, five going through [our company of soldiers] and two coming down the road toward me. . . . In a little less than two hours, 30 North Korean tanks rolled through the position we were supposed to block as if we hadn't been there. That was our first two hours in combat.[3]

The US soldiers' rocket launchers, known as bazookas, were no match for the North Koreans' Soviet tanks.

Soldiers discovered their 2.36-inch (5.99 cm) rocket launchers couldn't penetrate the thick armor of the T-34 tanks. According to one soldier, "Firing one of them at a tank was the same as throwing a rock at it."[5]

The US troops were also greatly outnumbered. Again and again the North Koreans hit head-on with tanks in massive

THE EDGE OF A VOLCANO

The United States knew about the tensions between North Korea and South Korea. So why wasn't the United States better prepared when war came? One US official compared the situation in Korea to living on the edge of a volcano: "We knew [Korea] would explode some day, but as day after day, month after month, and year after year passed and it did not blow up, we could hardly believe that tomorrow would be any different."[6]

frontal assaults. Then, the North Korean troops would move around the flanks, come up from behind, and cut off any possibility of US retreat. The inexperienced and poorly armed Task Force Smith could not possibly delay North Korea's advance. They needed additional assistance.

On July 7, the UN passed the US resolution to support South Korea. Truman chose General MacArthur as supreme commander of UN forces. Twenty countries besides the United States came to the aid of South Korea, either as combat units or to provide medical support. The UN had officially entered the war.

On July 19, 1950, President Truman addressed the nation, explaining the situation in Korea and what it could mean for Americans.

THE HORRORS OF WAR

By July 6, 1950, the UN force had increased to approximately 35,000 troops—10,000 US and 25,000 ROK. The North Koreans, however, had 90,000 troops.[1] Ground forces from other UN countries would not arrive until the end of August.

The first few weeks of the war were a disaster for UN troops. Weapons jammed, ammunition ran out, refugees clogged the roads, and scared troops got what was known as bugout fever, meaning they turned and ran rather than retreating in an organized fashion. UN troops were slowing the North Korean advance but not by much. North Korea was charging to the southern end of the peninsula. Things were desperate, and it seemed as though help would never come.

US soldiers landed in Pohang, South Korea, in July 1950. By midsummer, the US military was fully immersed in the Korean War.

TANKS

Both North Korea and the UN forces used tanks extensively during the Korean War. However, because of the narrow mountain passes common throughout South Korea, the destruction of one tank could cause a traffic jam of tanks and army vehicles for miles. One US soldier recalled seeing 788 destroyed trucks and tanks during a march from Taejon to Suwon, South Korea.

TOUGH TERRAIN

The landscape of Korea made ground combat especially difficult. Mountain and hills cover nearly 80 percent of the Korean Peninsula. For infantry, travel usually meant walking uphill or downhill. The small, winding roads were often little more than dirt paths that snaked through deep, narrow valleys. This was dangerous terrain for a soldier. Mountains could trap a fighting force and limit its movement. Troops and equipment were vulnerable to attack as enemy soldiers perched along the ridges and shot at them.

Similar to the North Korean forces, the UN forces relied heavily on a mechanized fighting force, including tanks, trucks, and mounted guns. These machines were tough to maneuver on winding mountain roads. The hills and mountains also made it difficult to find flat ground for the giant, cannonlike guns

The UN forces used tanks, such as this Sherman tank, in the Korean War, but the peninsula's rugged terrain often made maneuvering the tanks difficult.

known as mortars and howitzers. There was very little flat ground on the peninsula, and most flat ground was used for rice paddies, small flooded fields used to grow rice. In summer, the water-soaked ground was too soft to hold the heavy guns, and they would sink into the mud. In winter, the water in the

> **These kids of mine have all the guts in the world, and I can count on them to fight. But when they started out, they couldn't shoot. . . . They'd spent a lot of time listening to lectures on the difference between Communism and Americanism and not enough time crawling on their bellies on maneuvers with live ammunition singing over them. . . . They've had to learn in combat, in a matter of days, the basic things they should have known before they ever faced an enemy."[2]**
>
> — *US Colonel John "Iron Mike" Michaelis, commanding officer of the Twenty-Seventh Infantry Regiment*

ground froze, making it impossible to dig in the guns to hold them in place. These open fields also offered no protection from enemy fire.

Weather was another relentless enemy. During South Korea's humid summer heat, temperatures could rise as high as 105 degrees Fahrenheit (41°C). Men dropped from heat exhaustion and dehydration. Summer usually brought some relief in the form of monsoon rains. However, August 1950 brought a drought. The heat sapped the strength of already-exhausted men. Many drank from ditches that ran through the rice paddies and got violently sick because rice paddies were fertilized with human waste, and the water was contaminated.

At the beginning of the Korean War, most of the US soldiers in Korea came from MacArthur's peacetime force stationed in Japan. The conditions in Korea were a shock for these soldiers, who were used to the easy army life they had known in Japan. Many US troops thought they could storm into Korea and win in a few weeks. One soldier remembered, "Our officers told us to take our dress [noncombat] summer uniforms—we'd need them in a few weeks for the victory parade in Seoul."[3]

HELP ARRIVES

On July 14, additional US troops began arriving with new 3.5-inch (8.89 cm) rocket launchers capable of destroying T-34 tanks. General Walker, head commander on the ground for all US, UN, and ROK troops, established his headquarters in Korea on July 15. He now had roughly 18,000 US troops and 58,000 ROK troops under his command.[4] More troops and supplies began pouring in. During the last two weeks of July, 200 ships loaded with men and supplies arrived into the southern port city of Pusan. When units from other nations finally reached Korea, they too were assigned to Walker's Eighth Army. General MacArthur directed the overall war strategy from his base in Japan.

The fresh US forces delayed but did not stop the North Korean army storming southward down the peninsula. From July 19 to July 20, the city of Taejon, South Korea, 100 miles (161 km) south of Seoul, fell to the North Koreans. Once again, the North Koreans attacked from the front, moved around the flanks, and then surrounded the city.

After its victory at Taejon, North Korea split its force in two. One division moved south to the coast and then turned east. The rest of the North Korean force continued southeast toward Pusan. By the end of July 1950, the entire UN force was trapped in the small southeastern corner of Korea surrounding the port city of Pusan, which was serving as the temporary capital of South Korea.

HOLDING THE LINE

The Pusan Perimeter was an area approximately 50 miles (80 km) wide and 100 miles (161 km) long. To the east was the

It took the North Koreans less than two days to capture Taejon.

East Sea (Sea of Japan), and to the south was the Korean Strait. US naval power heavily protected both bodies of water. North of Pusan was a rugged mountain range, and the Naktong River lay to the west. The UN and ROK troops had nowhere to retreat, but with the US naval support and a relatively defendable position, Walker hoped his troops could hold their ground.

UN forces needed to defend a 140-mile (225 km) arc from the southwest to the northeast. On July 29, Walker told his troops:

> *There is no line behind us to which we can retreat. Every unit must counterattack to keep the enemy in a state of confusion and off balance. . . . We will fight as a team. If some of us must die, we will die fighting together. Any man who gives ground may be personally responsible for the death of thousands of his comrades. . . . I want everybody to understand that we are going to hold this line. We are going to win.[5]*

As Walker and his UN forces fought to defend the Pusan Perimeter, MacArthur prepared for Operation Chromite and the invasion of Inchon from his UN Command headquarters in Japan.

With UN strength increasing almost daily, North Korea knew it was now or never if it wanted to win the war. The North Korean army was split in two; its supply lines were stretching thinner and thinner. By early August, UN forces were at 100,000 troops.[6] Still, North Korean forces continually assaulted the Pusan Perimeter. On August 31, North Korean forces launched coordinated attacks in one last desperate onslaught.

Everywhere, the Pusan Perimeter seemed at risk of crumbling in what became known as the Battle of Pusan Perimeter. But North Korea's men, ammunition, and supplies couldn't hold up. The Pusan Perimeter held. The invasion of Inchon was imminent. North Korea had run out of time, and the UN was ready to take the offensive.

DESEGREGATING THE MILITARY

The Battle of Pusan Perimeter was one of the first major US battles fought by a desegregated US military group. In July 1948, Truman had issued Executive Order 9981, which prohibited racial and ethnic discrimination in the military. Prior to this time, black members of the armed services served in separate units from white troops. However, because of white opposition, integration within the armed services had not yet been implemented. During the Battle of Pusan Perimeter, US major general W. B. Kean placed approximately 250 black enlisted men with each white regiment, making up approximately 10 percent of each unit.[7] Kean reported that morale was good and in "many instances close friendships developed."[8] In 1954, the army abolished the last all-black military units, ending the practice of segregation.

THE TIDE TURNS

The retreat down the Korean Peninsula had been brutal for UN forces. The KPA was full of experienced fighters, most of whom had fought in the Chinese Communist revolution. However, UN forces had inflicted approximately 58,000 casualties between June 25 and early August.[1] UN forces also had vastly superior US air and naval power. The North Korean offensive was weakening. Yet UN forces still were under siege, defending positions rather than pushing forward.

INCHON AND SEOUL

In July 1950, MacArthur began considering an amphibious invasion in Korea to put UN forces on the offensive. On September 15, UN forces stormed Inchon with minimal resistance. The attack hit deep behind enemy lines, and the X Corps worked its way down toward Pusan, cutting off enemy

By early fall of 1950, the UN forces were ready to go on the offensive. The UN forces successfully captured Inchon on September 15.

> **"**No operation in military history can match . . . the brilliant maneuver which has now resulted in the liberation of Seoul. . . . Your transition from defensive to offensive operations was magnificently planned, timed and executed. . . . We remain completely confident that the great tasks entrusted to you by the United Nations will be carried to a successful conclusion."[5]
>
> —*President Truman, praising MacArthur's leadership at Inchon*

troops and supply lines as it went. At Seoul, the X Corps clashed with 20,000 North Korean troops sent to reinforce the city.[2]

The battle for Seoul was one of the most vicious battles of the entire war. The X Corps and North Korean fighters engaged in a street-by-street fight for the city. The KPA barricaded much of the city with tanks. US bombing attacks on KPA forces reduced almost the entire city to rubble.

By the evening of September 28, the X Corps had recaptured Seoul. On September 29, MacArthur turned the city over to a tearful Rhee: "In behalf of the United Nations command, I am happy to restore you, Mr. President, the seat of your government."[3] From the invasion of Inchon to Seoul, the X Corps suffered 3,500 casualties, most of them in Seoul. Roughly 14,000 North Koreans soldiers were killed and 7,000 captured.[4]

MacArthur restored Seoul to Rhee during a ceremony following the successful invasion of Seoul.

PUSAN BREAKOUT

With Almond's X Corps attacking the North Korean army from the rear, General Walker's Eighth Army was now ready to break out of Pusan. Walker knew the KPA's supply lines were overextended and their troop force was weakening. The KPA now had approximately 98,000 troops surrounding the Pusan

General Almond had told MacArthur he would recapture Seoul by September 25, exactly three months from the start of the war. Troops reached Seoul by September 25, but they did not secure the city for three more days. Seoul had roughly 2 million people at the start of the war. Many of these people were still in the city as the attack began. The fighting in Seoul was urban warfare—street by street and block by block. This was very different from what most UN soldiers had experienced, even those who had fought in World War II. Streets were blocked with tanks and chest-high barricades made from rice bags. In front of the barricades were antitank mines. Behind the barricades, North Koreans manned antitank and machine guns. Other North Korean soldiers hid in buildings and fired from windows and doors.

Marine Win Scott described his unit's leapfrog style of attack:

> *First we laid down as much fire as we could . . . Four guys, two on each side of the street, would . . . cover for each other. One group would fire into a building while the other two would work their way next to it. Then these*

UN troops shoot at North Korean forces from behind a barricade during the Battle of Seoul.

two would toss grenades through the windows to clear the inside and rush it. The teams would then reverse positions. The two who had taken the building would cover the other two across the street and the process would be repeated.[6]

UN forces finally liberated the city on September 28.

NORTH KOREAN SOLDIERS

At the start of the Korean War, approximately one-third of the North Korean troops had fought during the Communist revolution in China. These troops were battle-hardened and well trained. As the war progressed, however, troops were often inexperienced men and boys drafted into the army. The typical North Korean soldier had very little formal education and was accustomed to the harsh life of a peasant farmer. During the early years of the war, North Korean soldiers usually ate only one or two meals a day.

Perimeter compared to Walker's force of 156,500.[7] On September 16, the day after the invasion of Inchon, the Eighth Army began its offensive. It struggled to break out of the Pusan Perimeter. Ammunition was low. The soldiers lacked proper equipment to cross the river. Most important, the Eighth Army was already exhausted from two solid months of intense, continuous combat. However, on September 23, the KPA forces surrounding the Pusan Perimeter finally crumbled. The Eighth Army met up with the X Corps on September 26.

North Korean forces retreated northward. Some members of the North Korean army hid in the mountains as guerrilla fighters. However, by the end of September, there was no organized North Korean army in South Korea. It had been three months since the war started.

The UN originally entered the war because North Korea had crossed the 38th parallel into South Korean territory. Now North Korean forces were above the 38th parallel once more. UN leaders needed to make a decision. Should the UN forces end the fighting now? Or should they continue and push the Communists off the Korean Peninsula?

THE MISSION CHANGES

Rhee was not ready to quit. With UN forces supporting him, he saw his chance to rule a unified Korea. Rhee,

SERVICEWOMEN IN KOREA

At the time of the Korean War, women served in many branches of the US military. From 1950 to 1953, approximately 22,000 women were on active duty.[8] Approximately one-third of these were health professionals. Approximately half of the women served in personnel and administration, holding jobs such as radio operators, typists, stenographers, supply specialists, and drivers. Military jobs for servicewomen were restricted, as were promotions and higher ranks. Most of the US women serving in Korea were nurses. Nurses cared not only for injured troops but also for civilians, refugees, and the families of other US military personnel. They also helped set up and run hospitals. Military nurses often had to be flexible. Captain Viola McConnell was an army nurse assigned to help evacuate 643 American women and children from Korea. During the two-day journey, McConnell tended to a skull fracture, pneumonia, chicken pox, hernia, severe arthritis, one potential miscarriage, three labors and deliveries, five babies with diarrhea, and a senile elderly woman.

MacArthur, the Joint Chiefs of Staff, President Truman, other politicians, the media, and most US citizens also supported continuing the fight. The UN forces seemed to be on a roll. With hundreds of thousands of seemingly unstoppable troops, the UN forces might as well finish the job. This was their chance to finally push out the Communists and reunify Korea. Furthermore, an estimated 60,000 KPA troops still remained in North Korea.[9] If the UN pulled out, US officials reasoned, there would be nothing to prevent North Korea from simply attacking the South again.

On October 7, the UN made its decision. The UN mission in Korea had changed. The UN had previously hoped to contain Communism north of the 38th parallel. Now it was time to roll Communism out of the peninsula entirely.

The first UN troops crossed the 38th parallel on October 9, 1950, two days after the UN made its decision to push northward.

THE WAR MOVES NORTH

In just two weeks, the war had changed from tragedy to triumph for UN forces. Morale soared among the troops as well as Americans back home. With the smell of victory in the air, the mission had changed from containment to rollback. Although some UN members did not support UN forces operating north of the 38th parallel, the UN passed a resolution on October 7, 1959, recommending that Korea be unified.

Despite the new UN resolution, Truman did not want the war to spread. MacArthur had received new orders. His new military objective was to destroy the North Korean armed forces. However, Truman did not want MacArthur's troops engaging with the Chinese or Soviets. MacArthur could

After a string of victories in September, MacArthur, *left*, meeting with Truman, *right*, in October, was convinced the war was all but over.

> "We were sitting on a little hill eating C rations when down the road comes a couple of jeeps. . . . All these officers— we could see their eagles and stars—jumped out and began talking to the guys along the road. Here we were, sitting there eating, not knowing whether we should jump up and throw a salute or what. This one guy was real tall. He walked closer to us. It was General MacArthur. Boy, we were, you know, well, it was the thrill of a lifetime. MacArthur!"[1]

> —US Marine Doug Koch, describing the excitement of seeing General MacArthur

attack north of the 38th parallel as long as China and the Soviet Union did not enter North Korea or threaten to enter. UN forces were not to cross into Soviet or Chinese territory or air space. Additionally, MacArthur must use only ROK forces near the borders of the Soviet Union and China. Truman did not want to risk Americans accidentally crossing those borders.

A TWO-PRONGED APPROACH

MacArthur thought a two-pronged approach would be best, so he decided to keep the UN force divided. General Almond's X Corps would sail around the Korean Peninsula for an amphibious landing at the northeastern port of Wŏnsan, North Korea. Meanwhile, Walker's Eighth Army would move up along the western side of the peninsula to attack Pyongyang, the capital of North Korea. Both groups would then advance north toward the Yalu River, on the North Korea-China border.

A number of military leaders objected to MacArthur's plan. Keeping the UN force split diluted its strength and reduced the chance of rapid pursuit of the enemy. MacArthur ignored these objections. Military leaders had objected to his strategy at Inchon, but he had been right. He expected to prove them wrong again.

The UN assault slowed to a near standstill for three weeks as the X Corps and its supplies traveled to Wŏnsan. In the meantime, the Eighth Army and ROK troops were anxious to push ahead. ROK troops had crossed the 38th parallel on October 1 and captured Wŏnsan on October 10. Walker and his Eighth Army crossed the 38th parallel into North Korean territory on October 9 and captured Pyongyang on October 19. On October 24, MacArthur ordered

MacArthur planned an amphibious landing at Wŏnsan, but
first, navy divers known as frogmen had to clear thousands
of mines that littered the ocean floor near Wŏnsan.

his commanders to advance as quickly as possible. He wanted
to end the fighting before the onset of winter.

In the east, the X Corps sat waiting for mine sweepers to
clear approximately 3,000 explosive mines that blocked the

Wŏnsan coast. The X Corps did not land until October 26. Even the famous comedian Bob Hope, who came to entertain the troops, arrived in Wŏnsan before the X Corps did.

A WARNING FROM CHINA

The UN move into North Korean territory alarmed the Chinese. Back in September, when MacArthur returned Seoul to President Rhee, the Chinese foreign minister warned China would attack if UN forces moved into North Korea: "The Chinese people will not tolerate foreign aggression . . . [or] seeing their neighbor being savagely invaded."[3]

The United States thought China was bluffing. MacArthur insisted there

WAYS TO RELAX

The United Service Organizations Inc. (USO) was a nonprofit agency established by General George C. Marshall during World War II as a way of improving troop morale. The USO's goal was to provide social, recreational, and welfare programs for US troops and their families. USO shows, such as Bob Hope's performance in Wŏnsan, were especially popular as they brought celebrity entertainment to the troops. During the Korean War the military also offered a program called Rest and Recuperation (R&R). After six or seven months of combat, servicemen were rotated off the battle lines for five days of rest in Japan. R&R was intended to boost morale and reduce battle fatigue.

was very little chance of Chinese involvement. US officials still believed the attacks by North Korea on South Korea were Soviet-run operations. They underestimated China's influence on and involvement in North Korea. As a result, Americans did not take the Chinese threat seriously. This miscalculation would change the tide of the war.

CHINA GETS INVOLVED

The Chinese decided to intervene in Korea for several reasons. First, North Korean troops had fought in the Chinese Communist revolution. North Korean Communists had helped the Chinese; it was time to return the favor. Second, in the 1930s the Japanese had used Korea as a base to attack the Chinese region of Manchuria when Japan was still a US enemy. Japan was now a US ally, and the United States was an anticommunist country. China did not want a hostile foreign country right next door. Finally, by helping the North Koreans, China increased its influence on North Korea. Chinese leaders did not want the Soviet Union to have a dominant influence on their neighbor.

Actress Marilyn Maxwell, *left*, and comedian Bob Hope, *right*, entertained US troops in Wŏnsan as part of the USO program.

THE CHINESE INTERVENE

"On to the Yalu!" shouted ROK troops as they pushed northward in October 1950.[1] Led by South Korean general Paik Sun-yup, ROK troops raced ahead, anxious to unite all of Korea and win the war. On October 24, MacArthur ordered full use of all troops in North Korea, disregarding Truman's orders to use only ROK troops near the North Korea-China border. The Joint Chiefs of Staff overlooked this insubordination and did nothing to stop him.

SURPRISE ATTACKS

The push north had been speedy and relatively easy for UN forces. Some UN field commanders worried the advance had been too easy. They felt certain the enemy was luring

US Marines marched northward in November 1950.

GENERAL PAIK SUN-YUP

Paik Sun-yup was a South Korean army officer who became general and chief of staff of the South Korean army. He was also the commanding officer who discovered the Chinese had entered North Korea. From December 1951 to March 1952, Paik commanded a task force that successfully killed or captured more than 10,000 Communist guerrillas in South Korea.[2] Paik was known as an excellent combat commander.

them into a trap. Victory looked almost certain. Then something unexpected occurred. In the last week of October, enemy resistance suddenly stiffened. On October 25, the Eighth Army ROK unit led by General Paik captured a Chinese prisoner. This was the first time UN forces had solid proof the Chinese had entered Korea. More Chinese soldiers were spotted. More Chinese prisoners were taken. The extent of Chinese involvement was unclear, but over the next eight days, Chinese troops forced the Eighth Army to retreat south, first to Unsan, North Korea, and then to the Ch'ŏngch'ŏn River. On November 6, the Chinese broke contact and stopped attacking.

After landing at Wŏnsan on October 26, General Almond's X Corps moved up the coast and then inland toward the Yalu River and Chosin Reservoir. On November 2, Chinese forces attacked at Chosin. After four days of fierce fighting, UN forces eventually broke through Chinese resistance and came within a few miles of the reservoir. On November 6, the Chinese suddenly halted their advance and disappeared back into the mountains. They had given a warning. Now they were waiting to see how UN forces would react.

These Chinese attacks, known as the First Chinese Offensive, fundamentally changed the war, although UN commanders and troops did not know it yet. UN forces now realized Chinese troops were in Korea in large numbers, however they still second-guessed the reports

THE CHINESE SECRET WEAPON

Like KPA troops, Chinese troops were seasoned fighters who had fought during the Communist revolution in China and against the Japanese in the Sino-Japanese War (1932–1945). They carried supplies on their backs or by animal, so unlike the UN troops they were not forced to use the narrow roads that wound between the mountains and made soldiers vulnerable to enemy fire. In the winter, Chinese troops wore a thickly padded, quilted uniform, white on one side and khaki on the other, perfect camouflage for the snow. A thick, heavy cap with earmuffs protected the soldiers' heads and rubber sneakers helped them move silently during night marches. The Chinese troops had no heavy weapons, such as tanks. Despite their inferior weapons, the Chinese beat the UN forces. The skilled Chinese soldiers were able to move silently during night marches, which allowed them to take the UN troops by surprise.

Two US soldiers guard the front near the Yalu River.

of Chinese involvement. UN commanders thought the enemy soldiers were not really Chinese or that there were only a few scattered Chinese troops. MacArthur ignored the signs of trouble, convinced the Chinese and the battered remains of the KPA were not strong enough to launch an all-out offensive.

After November 6, the fighting quieted down for several weeks. MacArthur wanted to immediately resume the offensive. General Walker resisted. Unlike MacArthur, Walker feared this was no minor counterattack. Walker delayed any offensive movement while he resupplied his troops. On November 8, in an effort to slow the Chinese, MacArthur ordered the bombing of bridges that crossed the Yalu between North Korea and Manchuria.

DISASTER STRIKES

Winter was coming, and the UN forces were divided. They struggled with weak supply and communication lines, and now they were facing thousands of highly skilled and disciplined Chinese soldiers. Still, MacArthur insisted on pressing ahead. On November 23, the US troops celebrated Thanksgiving in Korea. The next day, on November 24, Walker launched his offensive, once again pushing north.

In the east, near the Chosin Reservoir, General Almond pressed the X Corps to advance as quickly as possible to the Yalu River. However, Almond's field commander, Major General Oliver P. Smith, worried they were marching into a trap. He deliberately tried slowing the advance. He also left piles of supplies along the way in case of retreat. Smith's careful planning would save thousands of lives. On November 27, the X Corps began its offensive near Chosin, fighting to break through enemy lines and push northward.

The enemy launched fierce counterattacks. UN forces were no match for the Chinese troops. UN commanders and troops had no idea the Chinese had amassed such a large force. There were 200,000 enemy troops fighting the Eighth Army, and 100,000 enemy troops fighting the X Corps.[3] Both groups of Chinese troops had slipped into North Korea from Manchuria largely undetected.

AN ENTIRELY NEW WAR

This was the beginning of the Second Chinese Offensive. The Chinese were pushing UN forces out of North Korea, giving the North Korean army a chance to regroup. On November 28, General MacArthur radioed the Joint Chiefs of Staff:

> *All hope of localization of the Korean conflict . . . can now be completely abandoned. . . . We face an entirely new war. . . . It is quite evident that our present strength of force is not sufficient. . . . This command has done everything humanly possible within its capabilities but is*

now faced with conditions beyond its control and its strength.[4]

The Eighth Army could not stop the waves of enemy troops. Many UN units were completely overrun, and chaos erupted as men fought to escape the Chinese soldiers. The Eighth Army was forced to fall back.

On November 29, MacArthur ordered Walker and the Eighth Army to retreat. They regrouped near Pyongyang, but on December 5 they were forced to retreat again. By mid-December, the Eighth Army had withdrawn south of the 38th parallel

AIR POWER

Throughout the Korean War, air power offered important support to ground forces. Bombers destroyed supply lines, cut off enemy movements, and attacked enemy positions before ground troops moved in. The North American F-86 Sabre was the most common fighter used by UN pilots. North Korean and Chinese pilots flew the Soviet-supplied MiG-15 fighters, and the Soviet Union eventually provided some pilots as well. UN pilots shot down more than 950 enemy aircraft during the war. US Air Force pilots shot down 900 of these. Enemy pilots shot down only 147 US-flown planes.[5] Because the UN force maintained air superiority throughout the war, almost all aerial combat took place over North Korea. Truman's mandate that UN forces could not cross into Soviet or Chinese airspace frustrated UN pilots. They wanted to chase the enemy. Instead they watched helplessly as enemy planes skirted across the border to safety.

Unable to defeat the well-trained and well-armed Chinese troops, the UN forces and ROK troops were forced to retreat from Pyongyang toward the 38th parallel.

to Seoul. The 130-mile (209 km) retreat was the longest in US military history.

On November 29, MacArthur also ordered Almond's X Corps to retreat from Chosin to the port of Hungnam.

The Battle of Chosin Reservoir was one of the most infamous and bitter battles of the Korean War. The X Corps evacuated by sea and returned to Pusan in early December.

By mid-December, UN forces had lost all the territory they had gained in North Korea. The victories at Inchon, MacArthur's promise of troops home by Christmas, Rhee's dream of a unified Korea—they had all been blown to smithereens.

TOUGH CONDITIONS

The winter of 1950 to 1951 was the coldest winter Korea had seen in 100 years. Temperatures fell to -25 degrees Fahrenheit (-32°C), making conditions extra difficult for the UN troops. Frozen ground made it impossible to dig protective shelters or level the ground for the large guns. Food and medicine froze. Medics thawed frozen syringes in their mouths. Fingers and toes turned black from frostbite. "Most of us had frozen tongues," said Marine James Ransone, Jr. "When we weren't fighting, we put our rifles next to our bodies to keep them from freezing."[6]

At the Chosin Reservoir, the 30,000 UN troops were no match for the 100,000 Chinese troops.[7] There was only one way in and one way out for the UN forces, a road known as the Main Supply Route (MSR). Chinese troops lined the road's 78-mile (126 km) length. When the Chinese severed the MSR in several places, the X Corps became trapped, cut off, and unable to retreat. US Major General Smith said, "You can't retreat or withdraw when you are surrounded. The only thing you can do is break out. When you break out, you attack. That's what we were doing."[8] The X Corps fought to break through the wall of Chinese forces for two weeks. Troops relied on Smith's stockpiles of supplies as they retreated. UN pilots provided air support. They bombed the enemy and dropped napalm, sometimes killing and injuring UN troops along with the Chinese. UN pilots also dropped supplies for the trapped X Corps. Eventually, the X Corps broke through the Chinese forces. On December 11, the last of the survivors reached Hungnam port in North Korea. According to Smith, 17,500 vehicles, 105,000 troops, and 91,000 refugees were evacuated back to Pusan on 109 ships.[9] To prevent the Chinese from using the port, UN forces completely destroyed it as they left.

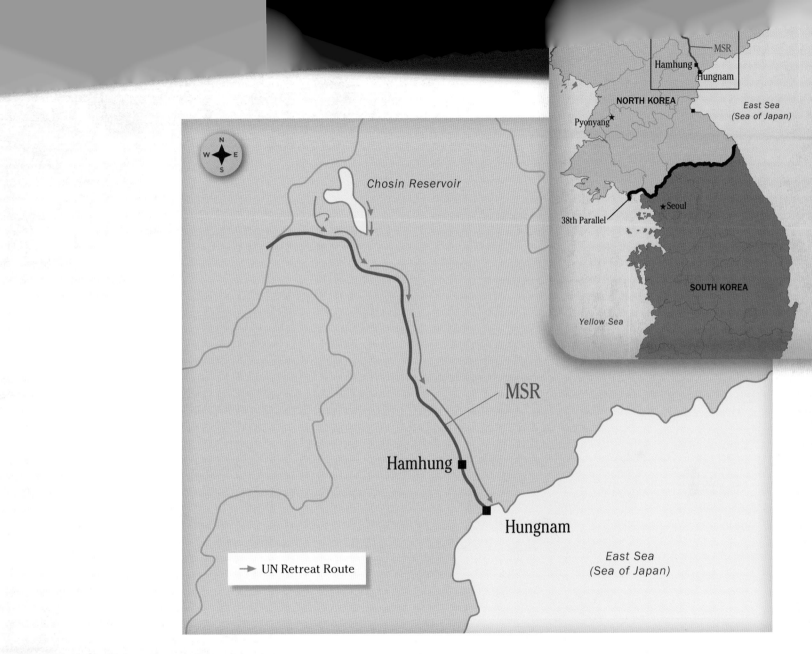

The UN retreat route along the MSR

SHATTERED FORCES

The winter of 1950 to 1951 was the lowest point of the war for UN forces. Victory had seemed so close just a few months ago. Troop morale was low. Many UN troops felt there was no way to beat the Chinese. There were too many Chinese troops, and they were too good. Stories of frozen, bloody battles and endless hordes of enemy soldiers created a desperate feeling. The situation seemed hopeless. Even the usually confident MacArthur was shaken by the massive failure of his November campaign. General Bradley of the Joint Chiefs of Staff said it was as if "MacArthur was throwing in the towel without the slightest effort to put up a fight. . . . Why hadn't MacArthur gone to Korea to steady Walker and rally the troops with his famous rhetoric? It was disgraceful."[1]

The harsh winter of 1950 to 1951 worsened the UN troops' already-low morale.

MacArthur argued for expanding the war. He requested more troops and suggested bombing Chinese factories and blockading the Chinese coast. He proposed that a line of radioactive waste be laid down between the Korean Peninsula and China. At age 70, MacArthur was near retirement. He did not want his military career to end with a massive failure.

Many Americans agreed that UN troops should keep pushing back against North Korea. However, Truman was adamant. He was not going to expand the war if he could avoid doing so, especially now that China was clearly involved. Going north to the Yalu River had been a disaster. Now the best Truman could hope for was damage control. Plans were made to evacuate Korea if necessary. Truman declared a national emergency. He feared the involvement of the Soviet Union and China could lead to yet another world war. If World War III was on its way, Truman wanted the United States to be ready.

RIDGWAY STEPS IN

On December 23, 1950, General Walker was killed in a jeep accident on an icy mountain road. General Matthew B. Ridgway took over the Eighth Army. The X Corps was discontinued as a unit, and its troops were once again part of the Eighth Army.

When Ridgway arrived in Korea on December 26, he found a defeated and discouraged army. Ridgway knew his troops could not win battles until morale improved.

Ridgway started with the basics: warmer clothes, better food, and better mobile army surgical hospitals (MASH) units. He rotated units out of combat for R&R, then rotated them back in. He insisted commanders lead by example. They must be at the front fighting where their men were.

The Eighth Army also needed to change its strategy. Ridgway insisted on patrolling the area to know where the enemy was and how large it was. The Eighth Army needed to get off the roads, hold high ground, and take the battle to the enemy.

Ridgway believed success started with the commanders. Good commanders led to

MASH UNITS

MASH units played an important role in treating injured soldiers during the Korean War. The first two MASH units arrived on July 6, 1950, just five days after Task Force Smith. Originally, the MASH units were intended to be mobile treatment facilities for up to 60 patients, but they soon expanded to 200-bed or more evacuation hospitals. Sometimes the units were set up in areas with no running water or electricity. One MASH unit was set up in an abandoned middle school, where the science lab became the operating room.

General Ridgway, *right*, brought strong leadership
and optimism to his command in 1951.

good fighting units. Ridgway instantly replaced commanders
who failed to meet his high standards.

US military leaders recognized Ridgway's strong leadership
skills. The Joint Chiefs of Staff began looking to Ridgway
instead of MacArthur. Unlike MacArthur, who consistently sent
negative reports about the situation in Korea, Ridgway said the
situation was improving. He was confident UN forces could hold

on. MacArthur was technically still supreme commander of the UN forces, but Ridgway was in charge.

THE THIRD CHINESE OFFENSIVE

By mid-December 1950, UN forces were below the 38th parallel and had formed a defensive perimeter around Seoul. The Chinese now faced the same choice Truman and the UN forces had faced a few months earlier—whether to cross the 38th parallel and try to unify the peninsula, or stop at the 38th parallel. The Chinese, too, decided to push forward.

On December 31, the Chinese launched massive attacks all along the front. On the eastern battlefront, North Korean forces broke through UN lines and moved southward to join guerrilla fighters. On the western battlefront, UN troops abandoned Seoul on January 4, 1951. It was like the beginning of the war all over again. Troops and refugees streamed southward, fleeing from the enemy. The Chinese pushed the Eighth Army 70 miles (113 km) south of the 38th parallel, and US officials feared the UN forces might have to evacuate the peninsula altogether.

ON THE OFFENSIVE AGAIN

Ridgway, however, was not so pessimistic. He realized the enemy troops, who carried their supplies on their backs or by animal, had a limited ability to maintain their supply lines. Under Ridgway's skillful command, UN forces once again took the offensive. Ridgway started with limited offensives to help restore confidence, then he moved to bigger campaigns. By the end of January, UN forces had carefully and cautiously resumed their advance northward. Their goal was to push the enemy north of the 38th parallel.

Operation Killer on February 21, was the first of a series of successful UN operations. Ridgway made it clear the goal was to push the Chinese as far north as possible, killing the maximum number of enemy troops, saying,

> War [is] concerned with killing the enemy. . . . I am by nature opposed to any effort to "sell" war to people as an only mildly unpleasant business that requires very little in the way of blood.[2]

UN forces recaptured Seoul on March 14, and by the end of March, they were back near the 38th parallel. Hoping to retake Seoul, 700,000 North Korean and Chinese forces launched a spring offensive against the 420,000 UN troops.[3] However, the superior numbers of Chinese troops were no match for the air and firepower of UN forces. In April, UN troops crossed the 38th parallel, but this time the United States had no intention of pushing Communism off the peninsula. They would leave North Korea as a Communist country. All major UN offensives stopped. The United States felt ready to negotiate a cease-fire.

A TOUGH DECISION

President Truman said sending troops into Korea was the hardest decision he ever made as president. But once Truman made the decision, he never wavered. When Truman ordered US troops to South Korea, more than 78 percent of Americans approved of his decision.[4] However, as bad news surrounding the Korean War poured in, Americans at home were dismayed. World War II had barely ended, and already US citizens were fighting and dying in a foreign land. Horrific images and terrible stories filled magazines and newspapers. By January 1951, 49 percent of Americans thought the US involvement in the Korean War was a mistake.[5]

MACARTHUR'S LAST STAND

MacArthur and Rhee, however, were not ready for a cease-fire. Rhee still wanted a unified Korea under his rule. To MacArthur, the Chinese were ruthlessly killing US troops, and it should be

STORIES FROM THE WAR

The Korean War often broke up families. Kim Chonggi, age 14, wrote this letter in 1951 from an orphanage in Seoul:

"I had a father but he left home in the earlier days of the war and nothing has been heard from him since. . . . I had a big brother but he went to join the National Army on the twenty-sixth of June last year and I have heard nothing of him since. . . . Whoever you are who receives this letter, I hope you will tell me something about my brother."

Chonggi later received a visit from his brother's best friend, Lieutenant Yi. Lieutenant Yi told Chonggi his brother had been killed at the front. Lying near Chonggi's dead brother was the body of another man, who had shot himself and was clutching a note:

"The note was scribbled in haste in ink. . . . With some difficulty, I read, 'Alas that a man should kill his own flesh-and-blood—even in war. . . . Kim Minhwan,'

My heart broke. It was Father's name. It was Father's handwriting."[6]

stopped. He wanted to invade China. The United States had nuclear weapons, and MacArthur wanted Truman to authorize dropping an atomic bomb on China. He believed such an action would win the war and help rid the world of Communism at the same time. However, Truman made it clear the United States had no intention of directly attacking China.

MacArthur made deliberately provocative statements criticizing Truman's policies. The final straw was a publicized letter by MacArthur. The letter was read on the floor of Congress on April 5. MacArthur wrote,

> *If we lose the war to Communism in Asia the fall of Europe is inevitable, win it and Europe most probably would avoid war and yet preserve freedom. . . . There is no substitute for victory.*[7]

On April 11, newspapers shocked the world with the headline "Truman Fires MacArthur."[8] In a radio address that day, Truman explained his actions:

> *In the simplest terms, what we are doing in Korea is this: We are trying to prevent a third world war. . . . Why don't we bomb Manchuria and China itself? . . . [we] would be running a very grave risk of starting a general war. . . . Behind the North Koreans and Chinese Communists in the*

front lines stand additional millions of Chinese soldiers.
And behind the Chinese stand the tanks, the planes, the
submarines, the soldiers, and the scheming rulers of
the Soviet Union. Our aim is to avoid the spread of the
conflict.[9]

Despite Truman's words, many Americans agreed with MacArthur. The general was a popular war hero from World War II, and most Americans harbored anticommunist attitudes. Support for Truman plummeted. Many Americans thought Truman was the one who should be fired, and some even called for the president to be impeached and removed from office.

MOVE TO ARMISTICE

On June 30, with approval from Truman, General Ridgway radioed a message to the commander in chief of Communist forces. In the message, he proposed a meeting to discuss a cease-fire. Ridgway received a response on July 1:

After consultations held today between General Kim
Il-Sung, commander in chief of the Korean army, and
General Peng De-huai, commander in chief of the Chinese
Peoples Volunteers . . . We are authorized to tell you
that we agree to suspend military activities and to hold

Many US soldiers and citizens disagreed with Truman's decision to remove MacArthur from his command. MacArthur returned home to fanfare and parades.

peace negotiations, and that our delegates will meet with yours.[10]

After one year of fighting, it looked as if the war was going to end.

A LONG, BITTER END

Neither Kim Il-Sung nor Syngman Rhee got what they wanted from the Korean War: a unified Korea, ruled by Koreans under one political system. Yet neither side could continue fighting without support from their foreign allies, and the allies wanted to end the war.

The Chinese agreed to suspend military activities during the peace negotiations, but Ridgway and other US officials were suspicious. If military activities ceased during negotiations, it would give the Chinese time to build up their military force. The United States believed the Chinese were preparing for another offensive. The Joint Chiefs of Staff responded to the Chinese message agreeing to talks but saying

The UN negotiating team prepares to meet the Communists for peace talks in July 1951.

nothing about suspending military activities. The fighting would continue, even while the two sides discussed peace.

THE NEGOTIATION ROLLERCOASTER

On July 10, 1951, cease-fire negotiations began in the South Korean city of Kaesong. The negotiations went on for much longer than anyone anticipated. The main disagreements were the demarcation line, which would be the new border between North Korea and South Korea, withdrawal of foreign troops, and the exchange of prisoners. The US-South Korean delegation wanted a demilitarized zone along current battle lines and an inspection team to monitor troops and weapons buildups. The Chinese-North Korean delegation wanted withdrawal of all foreign troops from the Korean Peninsula. The US-South Korean delegation feared total withdrawal would permit China to send troops into North Korea later. The talks went nowhere, and in August, China and North Korea broke off negotiations.

On October 25, talks began once again, this time in Panmunjom, which sits on the border of North and South Korea. The United States had originally agreed to an immediate exchange of prisoners of war (POWs) once a cease-fire agreement was signed. But nearly half of the North Korean

Trench-style warfare continued throughout the peace talks because of the United States' refusal to suspend military activities.

POWs did not want to return to North Korea, and Truman did not want to force them to. By October 1952, one year after peace talks had restarted, no progress had been made. This time, the US-South Korean negotiators walked out.

Because of the United States' unwillingness to suspend military activities during peace talks, fighting continued the entire time. This fighting involved trench warfare as both sides fought for minor positions that made little difference to the negotiations. The loss of life that occurred after peace talks began was far greater than losses before the talks, even though there were no major battles.

Talks resumed again in April 1953. This time, Rhee was the sticking point. He still clung to his dream of a Korea united and under his rule. He even threatened to go to war against North Korea on his own. In an effort to disrupt negotiations, Rhee freed 25,000 North Korean POWs who should have been returned to North Korea once the cease-fire agreement was signed.[1] Not wanting to return to the North, these POWs disappeared into the South Korean countryside. In the end, Rhee accepted the cease-fire agreement, but he refused to sign it. On July 27, 1953, at 10:00 a.m., delegates from both sides signed the agreement. The truce between North Korea and South Korea officially went into effect at 10:00 p.m. that night.

THE PRICE OF WAR

The war took a terrible toll on the armed forces of all sides, but an even greater toll on the people of Korea. Statistics on casualties from the war vary widely, but the Korean War likely caused more than 4 million Korean casualties. At least 2 million of these casualties were civilians.[2] Most of Korea was reduced to rubble. All sides in the war were guilty of atrocities. POWs were killed. In one case, US prisoners were found shot dead in a ditch, their hands tied behind them with barbed wire. US troops sometimes panicked and killed civilians. Entire villages in both countries were wiped out because they might harbor the enemy. Thousands of political prisoners were also killed, particularly in South Korea. One Central Intelligence Agency agent described seeing two bulldozers digging a ditchlike grave, then truckloads of political prisoners arrived, were shot in the head, and pushed into the grave.

The US Air Force dropped 476,000 tons (432,000 metric tons) of bombs on roads, railways, power plants, dams, industrial centers, airfields, and enemy troops. The bombing of dams at Kusong and Toksan, North Korea, in May 1953, were particularly devastating. Whole villages were washed away, the rice crop was largely destroyed, and flash flooding wiped out railways, highways, and bridges. Nevertheless, airpower never completely stopped the enemy's movement.

> **❝** [There were] no more cities in North Korea: . . . there was only devastation . . . I don't know why houses collapsed and chimneys did not, but I went through a city of 200,000 inhabitants and I saw thousands of chimneys and that—that was all."[3]
>
> —Tibor Meray, Hungarian war correspondent

NEVER FORGET

The Korean War is sometimes known as the Forgotten War in the United States because it has gotten less attention in recent years than the more widely publicized wars that preceded and followed it—World War II and the Vietnam War (1954–1975). Although the Korean War stopped the spread of Communism in South Korea, the war ended in a stalemate. North Korea and South Korea remained divided, and the border between them was roughly where it had been before the war. It seemed as if the war had accomplished very little.

Because he feared the war could escalate into World War III, President Truman had insisted on a limited war with limited aims. However, many Americans had felt that if they were going to fight, they should fight to win. Dissatisfaction with the Korean War and Truman's policies played an important role in the election of Republican president Dwight D. Eisenhower in November 1952. Truman decided not to run again, so Eisenhower ran against Democratic candidate Adlai E. Stevenson. Many historians see Eisenhower's overwhelming victory over Stevenson as a reflection of the public's opinion on the Democratic Truman administration. China's role in the Korean War led President Eisenhower to push for tougher policies toward China.

STORIES FROM THE WAR

US Corporal Robert Hall described the scene the morning after the armistice agreement was signed, when the war was finally over:

"At earliest light the troops came up out of the ground to look. . . . It was unheard of—standing in the open in daylight. An incredible feeling. I think the infantrymen all across the peninsula, on both sides of the line, must have been awed by it. Just the simple, natural act of standing erect in the sunshine. Then to look, and eventually to walk through the land ahead of the trenches, something that would have meant sure death twenty-four hours before. That's when we began to realize that it was really over."[4]

The Korean War Memorial in Washington, DC, helps
honor US troops' roles in the Korean War.

The Korean War added fuel to the Cold War between the
United States and the Soviet Union, and it was the beginning
of the military arms race between the two countries. Tensions
between the United States and the Soviet Union remained high
for another 40 years. US fears over the spread of Communism

also contributed to the Vietnam War.

The Korean War has certainly not been forgotten by North Korea, South Korea, or China. On all sides, the fighters were fighting for something they believed in. Both North and South Korea wanted a unified country. Chinese forces came to the aid of a neighbor who had helped them. Americans fought to prevent the spread of oppressive governments. To those who witnessed and experienced the war, the Korean War can never be forgotten.

KOREAN PAWNS

As many as 4 million Koreans were killed in the Korean War, at least half of these were civilians.[5] According to historian William Stueck, "Korea's ultimate fate was determined abroad, this time in Moscow, Washington, and Beijing by leaders to whom Korea was merely a pawn on a crowded international chessboard."[6]

1945

World War II ends. The United States divides the Korean Peninsula.

1950

North Korea launches a major assault against South Korea on June 25.

1950

Task Force Smith, the first US ground troops, arrive in Korea on July 1.

1950

UN forces liberate Seoul, the capital of South Korea, on September 28.

1950

In October, UN forces cross the 38th parallel. The UN's mission shifts from defense of South Korea to the destruction of the North Korean regime.

1950

UN forces take the North Korean capital of Pyongyang on October 19.

1950

Chinese troops attack UN forces in the First Chinese Offensive on October 25.

1950

On November 28, UN forces begin retreating south.

1950

General Matthew B. Ridgway takes command of UN ground forces on December 26.

1951

UN forces recapture Seoul on March 14.

1951

President Harry S. Truman fires General Douglas MacArthur on April 11.

1951

Cease-fire negotiations begin on July 10.

1953

On July 27, an armistice is signed at Panmunjom. Both sides withdraw slightly to create a demilitarized zone between North Korea and South Korea.

KOREAN WAR BATTLES, 1950–1953

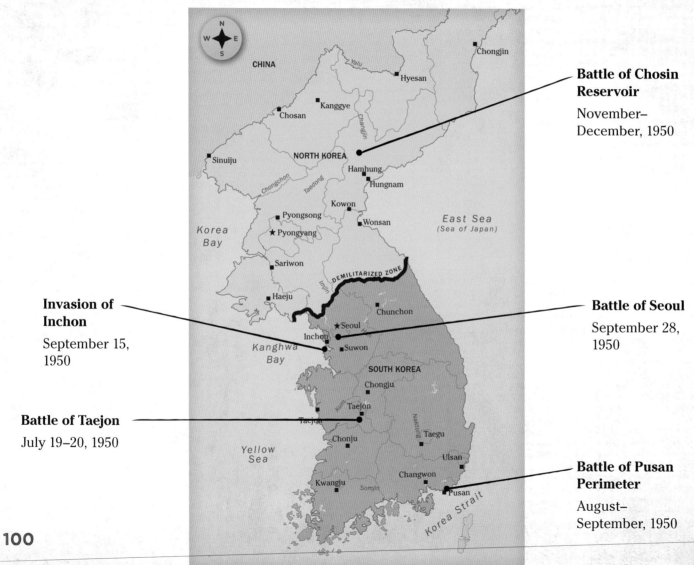

Battle of Chosin Reservoir

November–December, 1950

Battle of Seoul

September 28, 1950

Invasion of Inchon

September 15, 1950

Battle of Taejon

July 19–20, 1950

Battle of Pusan Perimeter

August–September, 1950

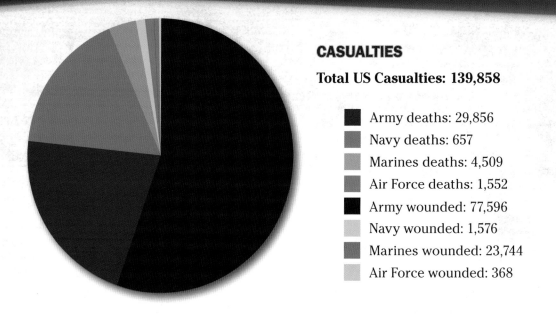

CASUALTIES

Total US Casualties: 139,858

- Army deaths: 29,856
- Navy deaths: 657
- Marines deaths: 4,509
- Air Force deaths: 1,552
- Army wounded: 77,596
- Navy wounded: 1,576
- Marines wounded: 23,744
- Air Force wounded: 368

KEY PLAYERS

General Douglas MacArthur was the supreme commander of the United Nations troops until he was fired in April 1951.

Harry S. Truman was president of the United States from 1945 to 1953, including most of the Korean War.

Kim Il-Sung was the Communist leader of North Korea.

Syngman Rhee was the president of South Korea.

General Matthew B. Ridgway took command of the Eighth Army in December 1950. He eventually replaced MacArthur as the supreme commander of the UN forces during the last few years of the Korean War.

GLOSSARY

amphibious
Executed by coordinated action of land, sea, and air forces organized for invasion.

artillery
Large weapons used to fire long-range explosives.

cease-fire
The suspension of military activities.

Cold War
The hostile relationship between the Soviet Union, the United States, and their allies after World War II, marked by military buildups and political conflict, but without actual military attacks.

Communism
A political system in which the government controls all political, economic, and social activity.

guerrilla
A fighter that combats the enemy without using standard military tactics.

infantry
Soldiers trained to fight on foot.

napalm

Oil or gas in a gel form and used in bombs.

offensive

A major military attack carried out by a large number of soldiers for the purpose of capturing territory.

segregation

Separating groups of people based on race, gender, ethnicity, or other factors.

United Nations (UN)

An international organization of countries that work together to promote international law, human rights, and economic development.

SELECTED BIBLIOGRAPHY

Cumings, Bruce. *The Korean War: A History*. New York: Modern Library, 2010. Print.

Halberstam, David. *The Coldest Winter: America and the Korean War*. New York: Hyperion, 2007. Print.

James, D. Clayton, and Anne Sharp Wells. *Refighting the Last War: Command and Crisis in Korea 1950–1953*. New York: Free Press, 1993. Print.

FURTHER READINGS

English, June A., and Thomas D. Jones. *Scholastic Encyclopedia of the United States at War*. New York: Scholastic, 2003. Print.

Foran, Raquel. *North Korea*. Minneapolis: ABDO, 2013. Print.

Foran, Raquel. *South Korea*. Minneapolis: ABDO, 2013. Print.

WEB SITES

To learn more about the Korean War, visit ABDO Publishing Company online at **www.abdopublishing.com**. Web sites about the Korean War are featured on our Book Links page. These links are routinely monitored and updated to provide the most current information available.

PLACES TO VISIT

Korean War Memorial

10 Daniel French Drive Southwest
Washington, DC, 20001
202-426-6841
http://www.nps.gov/kowa/index.htm
The Korean War Veterans Memorial honors members of the US Armed
Forces who served in the Korean War.

Smithsonian Air and Space Museum

14390 Air and Space Museum Parkway
Chantilly, VA 20151
703-572-4118
http://www.airandspace.si.edu/exhibitions/uhc/es_korea_vietnam_
aviation.cfm
Fighter and bomber planes were used during the Korean War to support
ground troops and attack enemy supply lines. Airplanes in the *Korea
and Vietnam Aviation* exhibit include the F-4S Phantom, A-6E Intruder,
F-86A Sabre, and the Russian MiG-15.

Truman Presidential Library and Museum

500 West US Highway 24
Independence, MO 64050
1-800-833-1225
http://www.trumanlibrary.org
The Harry S. Truman Library and Museum contains exhibits about
Truman's life and presidency.

CHAPTER 1. A BOLD PLAN

1. James I. Matray. "Revisiting Korea: Exposing Myths of the Forgotten War, Part I." *Prologue Magazine* 34.1 (2002). *National Archives*, n.d. Web. 18 Mar. 2013.

2. Adrian R. Lewis. *The American Culture of War: The History of U.S. Military Force from World War II to Operation Iraqi Freedom.* New York: Routledge, 2007. Print. 98.

3. Bevin Alexander. *Korea: The First War We Lost.* New York: Hippocrene, 1998. Print. 159–160.

4. Adrian R. Lewis. *The American Culture of War: The History of U.S. Military Force from World War II to Operation Iraqi Freedom.* New York: Routledge, 2007. Print. 98–99.

5. Bruce Cumings. *Korea's Place in the Sun: A Modern History.* New York: Norton, 2005. Print. 276.

6. Bevin Alexander. *Korea: The First War We Lost.* Rev. ed. New York: Hippocrene, 1998. Print. 217.

7. D. Clayton James and Anne Sharp Wells. *Refighting the Last War: Command and Crisis in Korea 1950–1953.* New York: Free Press, 1993. Print. 173.

CHAPTER 2. A DIVIDED NATION

1. David McCullough. *Truman.* New York: Simon, 1992. Print. 546–547.

2. Bruce Cumings. *The Korean War: A History.* New York: Modern Library, 2010. Print. 66.

3. Richard W. Stewart, Ed. *American Military History Volume II.* Washington, DC: Center of Military History United States Army, 2005. PDF. 219.

4. "'A Report to the National Security Council – NSC 68' President's Secretary's File, Truman Papers." *Trumanlibrary.org.* Harry S. Truman Library and Museum, 12 Apr. 1950. Web. 18 Dec. 2012. PDF. 4.

5. Ibid. 6.

6. Kim Il Sung. "Korea Must Be Reunified." *Living Through the Korean War.* Ed. Charles W. Carey, Jr. Farmington Hills, MI: Thomson Gale, 2006. Print. 25.

7. John J. Muccio. "Memorandum from the State Department to Harry S. Truman, June 24, 1950." *Trumanlibrary.org.* Harry S. Truman Library and Museum, n.d. Web. 12 Dec. 2012.

CHAPTER 3. THE UNITED STATES STEPS IN

1. David McCullough. *Truman*. New York: Simon, 1992. Print. 775.
2. Donald Knox. *The Korean War, Pusan to Chosin: An Oral History*. New York: Harcourt, 1985. Print. 13.
3. Ibid. 20.
4. Richard W. Stewart, Ed. *American Military History Volume II*. Washington, DC: Center of Military History United States Army, 2005. PDF. 223.
5. Donald Knox. *The Korean War, Pusan to Chosin: An Oral History*. New York: Harcourt, 1985. Print. 38.
6. William Stueck. *The Korean War: An International History*. Princeton, NJ: Princeton UP, 1995. Print. 11.

CHAPTER 4. THE HORRORS OF WAR

1. David McCullough. *Truman*. New York: Simon, 1992. Print. 787.
2. Max Hastings. *The Korean War*. New York: Simon, 1987. Print. 95–96.
3. Donald Knox. *The Korean War, Pusan to Chosin: An Oral History*. New York: Harcourt, 1985. Print. 11.
4. Roy Edgar Appleman. *United States Army in the Korean War, Volume 1*. Washington, DC: Government Printing Office, 1987. Print. 110.
5. Donald Knox. *The Korean War, Pusan to Chosin: An Oral History*. New York: Harcourt, 1985. Print. 72–73.
6. David McCullough. *Truman*. New York: Simon, 1992. Print. 796.
7. Sherie Mershon and Steven Schlossman. *Foxholes & Color Lines: Desegregating the U.S. Armed Forces*. Baltimore: Johns Hopkins UP, 1998. Print. 226.
8. Ibid.

CHAPTER 5. THE TIDE TURNS

1. Max Hastings. *The Korean War*. New York: Simon, 1987. Print. 82.
2. Bevin Alexander. *Korea: The First War We Lost*. New York: Hippocrene, 1998. Print. 217.
3. Ibid. 216–217.
4. D. Clayton James and Anne Sharp Wells. *Refighting the Last War: Command and Crisis in Korea 1950–1953*. New York: Free Press, 1993. Print. 173.
5. Ibid. 175.

6. Donald Knox. *The Korean War, Pusan to Chosin: An Oral History*. New York: Harcourt, 1985. Print. 289–290.

7. Spencer C. Tucker. *Battles that Changed History: An Encyclopedia of World Conflict*. Santa Barbara, CA: ABC-CLIO, LLC, 2011. Print. 559.

8. Linda Witt et al. *"A Defense Weapon Known to Be of Value": Servicewomen of the Korean War Era*. Lebanon, NH: UP of New England, 2005. Print. 33.

9. Richard W. Stewart, Gen Ed. *American Military History Volume II*. Washington, DC: Center of Military History United States Army, 2005. PDF. 229.

CHAPTER 6. THE WAR MOVES NORTH

1. Donald Knox. *The Korean War, Pusan to Chosin: An Oral History*. New York: Harcourt, 1985. Print. 263.

2. David McCullough. *Truman*. New York: Simon, 1992. Print. 807.

3. Adrian R. Lewis. *The American Culture of War: The History of U.S. Military Force from World War II to Operation Iraqi Freedom*. New York: Routledge, 2007. Print. 102.

CHAPTER 7. THE CHINESE INTERVENE

1. David Halberstam. *The Coldest Winter: America and the Korean War*. New York: Hyperion, 2007. Print. 14.

2. Paul M. Edwards. *Combat Operations of the Korean War: Ground, Air, Sea, Special and Covert*. Jefferson, NC: McFarland, 2010. Print. 70.

3. David Halberstam. *The Coldest Winter: America and the Korean War*. New York: Hyperion, 2007. Print. 309–310.

4. Roy Edgar Appleman. *East of Chosin: Entrapment and Breakout in Korea, 1950*. Williams-Ford, TX: Texas A&M UP, 1987. Print. 168–169.

5. Harry G. Summers, Jr., ed. *Korean War Almanac*. New York: Facts on File, 1991. Print. 39–40.

6. Donald Knox. *The Korean War, Pusan to Chosin: An Oral History*. New York: Harcourt, 1985. Print. 551.

7. Walter T. Ham IV, Eighth Army Public Affairs. "Veterans Mark 60th Anniversary of Reservoir Battle." *United State Forces Korea*. USFK Public Affairs Office, n.d. Web. 18 Mar. 2013.

8. Donald Knox. *The Korean War, Pusan to Chosin: An Oral History*. New York: Harcourt, 1985. Print. 531.

9. Ibid. 613.

CHAPTER 8. SHATTERED FORCES

1. David Halberstam. *The Coldest Winter: America and the Korean War*. New York: Hyperion, 2007. Print. 477.

2. Ibid. 490.

3. Maurice Isserman. *Korean War*. Ed. John S. Bowman. New York: Facts on File, 2003. Print. 90.

4. Steve Crabtree. "The Gallup Brain: Americans and the Korean War." *GALLUP*. Gallup, 4 Feb. 2003. Web. 18 Mar. 2013.

5. Ibid.

6. Kim Chonggi. "A Tombstone for Three." *6 Insides from the Korean War*. Seoul, Korea: Dae-Dong Moon Hwa Sa, 1958. Print. 73, 78–79.

7. David McCullough. *Truman*. New York: Simon, 1992. Print. 838.

8. Ibid. 843.

9. Harry S. Truman. *Harry S. Truman: The Man From Missouri, The Memorable Words of the Thirty-Third President*. Ed. Ted Sheldon. Kansas City, MO: Hallmark, 1970. Print. 14.

10. Bevin Alexander. *Korea: The First War We Lost*. New York: Hippocrene, 1998. Print. 428–429.

CHAPTER 9. A LONG, BITTER END

1. Max Hastings. *The Korean War*. New York: Simon, 1987. Print. 322–323.

2. Bruce Cumings. *The Korean War: A History*. New York: Modern Library, 2010. Print. 35.

3. Ibid. 158–159.

4. Donald Knox and Alfred Coppel. *The Korean War, Uncertain Victory: The Concluding Volume of an Oral History*. New York: Harcourt, 1988. Print. 504–505.

5. Bruce Cumings. *The Korean War: A History*. New York: Modern Library, 2010. Print. 243.

6. William Stueck. *The Korean War: An International History*. Princeton, NJ: Princeton UP, 1995. Print. 51.

ABOUT THE AUTHOR

Shannon Baker Moore is a freelance writer and editor who writes for both adults and children. A college writing instructor, she is a member of the Society of Children's Book Writers and Illustrators and the Missouri Writers' Guild. She and her family have lived throughout the United States and currently live in Saint Louis, Missouri.